LIFE'S LITTLE BOOK OF

comfort
AND JOY

JO PETTY

BRISTOL PARK BOOKS

Published by:

BRISTOL PARK BOOKS, INC.

252 W. 38th Street, New York, NY 10018

Previously published by Bristol Park Books in 2012
This edition published by Bristol Park Books in 2016

Bristol Park Books is a registered trademark of Bristol Park Books, Inc.

Library of Congress Control Number: 2012939555
ISBN: 978-0-88486-617-6   E Book ISBN: 978-0-88486-619-0

Cover and text design by LaBreacht Design
Printed in Malaysia

foreword

CULLED FROM MANY different sources, these eloquent
and heartfelt praises celebrate the basic Christian virtues
—faith, long suffering, meekness, temperance—that have
served as a cornerstone for all my devotional works.

These writings have been a constant source of inspiration
and spiritual sustenance to me in my daily life, and I share
them with you, my beloved readers, in the hope that they
will set your hearts singing and spirits soarings.

—Jo Petty

contents

Love

Work is
love made
visible.

To love is virtually to know;
to know is not virtually to love.

Do not judge your friend
until you stand in his place.

Except in occasional emergencies, there
is not much that one man can do for another,
other than to help him help himself.

It is only the forgiving
who are qualified
to receive forgiveness.

A friend is a person with whom
you dare to be yourself.

Love is not soft like water, it is hard like a rock,
on which the waves of hatred beat in vain.

Mrs.—Do you love me still?
Mr.—Yes, better than any other way.

We like someone because.
We love someone although.

Always forgive your enemies;
nothing annoys them so much.

A friend is a present you give yourself.

Friends are made by many acts—
and lost by only one.

Politeness is a small price to pay
for the good will and affection of others.

It is better to have loved and lost
than never to have loved at all.

Every calling is great
when greatly pursued.

Mothers, as well as fools,
sometimes walk where angels fear to tread.

'Twas her thinking of others
made you think of her.

Some women work so hard
to make good husbands that they never
quite manage to make good wives.

Love is the root
of all virtues.

The greatest happiness of life is the conviction
that we are loved, loved for ourselves,
or rather loved in spite of ourselves.

If nobody loves you, be sure it is your fault.

Love understands, and love waits.

Not where I breathe, but where I love, I live.

I hold him great who for love's sake
Can give with earnest, general will.
But he who takes for love's sweet sake,
I think I hold more generous still.

The remedy for wrongs is to forget them.

Love your enemies,
for they tell you your faults.

He who despises, despises not men,
but God.

Science has made the world a neighborhood,
but it will take religion to make it a brotherhood.

Increase and abound in love, one toward another,
and toward all men.

We cannot give like God, but surely
we may forgive like Him.

There are shadow friendships that appear
only when the sun shines.

Bless the Lord, O my soul: and all that is
within me, bless His holy name.

I shall love the Lord my God with all my heart,
and with all my soul, and with all my mind.
This is the first commandment.
And the second is like, namely this,
I shall love my neighbor as myself.
There are no commandments greater than these.

Wear a breastplate of faith and love;
and for a helmet, the hope of salvation.

If I judge not and condemn not,
I shall not be judged nor condemned.

Love never fails.

Love endures all things.

He that spares his rod hates his son:
but he that loves him chastens him.

Love is the greatest thing
in the world!

No person is outside
the scope of God's love.

Hatred is like an acid. It can do more
damage to the vessel from which it is stored
than to the object on which it is poured.

Love behaves.

Do I love things and use people
or love people and use things?

Love can't be wasted.

A cheerful friend is like a sunny day.

Love hears what the ear cannot.

Friendship is to be purchased
only by friendship.

A foreigner is a friend I haven't met yet.

Go often to the house of your friend,
for weeds choke up the unused path.

To learn and never
be filled, is wisdom;
To teach and never
be weary is love.

Love praises others.

The best way for a husband to clinch an argument
is to take her in his arms.

The language of love is understood by all.

Love is kind.

Come what may, hold fast to love!
Though men should rend your heart,
let them not embitter or harden it.
We win by tenderness;
we conquer by forgiveness.

Love is the law of life.

To understand is to pardon.

The smallest good deed
is better than the
grandest intention.

The best gifts are tied with heartstrings.

A friend is one who comes to you
when all others leave.

Success in marriage is much more
than finding the right person;
it is a matter of being the right person.

Let us love in deed
and in truth
rather than in word
and tongue.

We must love our fellow man because
God loves him and wills to redeem him.

If there is anything better than to be loved,
it is loving.

What counts is not the number of hours you put in,
but how much you put in the hours.

The heart has reasons
that reason
does not understand.

Teach me, Father, when I pray,

Not to ask for more,

But rather let me give thanks

For what is at my door.

For food and drink, for gentle rain,

For sunny skies above,

For home and friends, for peace and joy,

But most of all for LOVE.

The coin of God's realm is love.

Charity gives itself rich;
covetousness hoards itself poor.

God sent not His Son into the world
to condemn the world;
but that the world through Him might be saved.

God pardons like a mother,
who kisses the offense
into everlasting forgiveness.

Real friends are those who,
when you've made a fool of yourself,
don't feel that you've done a permanent job.

Faults are thick when love is thin.

You shall judge a man by his foes
as well as by his friends.

God loves me in spite of my faults.

Support the weak and cheer the fainthearted.

To whom little is forgiven, the same loves little.

Love is willing to wait.

JOY

Little and often
fills the purse.

Keep your enthusiasms, and forget your birthdays—
formula for youth!

Money and time are the heaviest of burdens of life,
and the unhappiest of all mortals are those
who have more of either than they know how to use.

Joy, temperance and repose
Slam the door on the doctor's nose.

Keep on your toes and you won't run down at the heels.

Happiness is a perfume you cannot pour on others
without getting a few drops on yourself.

To be without some of the things you want
is an indispensable part of happiness.

The worst bankrupt in the world
is the man who has lost his enthusiasm.
Let him lose everything but enthusiasm
and he will come through again to success.

For all its terrors and tragedies… the life of man
is a thing of potential beauty and dignity….
To live is good.

What one has, one ought to use;
and whatever he does he should do with all his might.

An unfailing mark of a block head
is the chip on his shoulder.

Any person who is always feeling sorry for himself,
should be.

It is not he who has little,
but he who wants more, who is poor.

Old age isn't so bad…
when you consider the alternative.

Mirth is from God, and dullness is from the devil.
You can never be too sprightly,
you can never be too good-tempered.

To be happy ourselves is a most effectual contribution
to the happiness of others.

The world belongs to the enthusiast who keeps cool.

Blessed is the man who digs a well
from which another may draw faith.

Every man's work
is a portrait of himself.

One great use of words is to hide our thoughts.

To see God in everything makes life
the greatest adventure there is.

Happiness is the best teacher of good manners;
only the unhappy are churlish.

O, I am grown so free from care
since my heart broke!

Optimist or Pessimist?
So you call traffic signals go-lights?

Sympathy is never wasted
except when you give it to yourself.

To be wronged
is nothing unless
you continue
to remember it.

Visits always give pleasure—
if not the coming, then the going.

Joy is not in things, it is in us.

Almost all men improve on acquaintance.

If you don't make a living, live on what you make.

Success is getting what you want;
Happiness is wanting what you get.

The deeper that sorrow carves into your being,
the more joy you can contain.

It is when the holiday is over
that we begin to enjoy it.

Pleasures are like poppies spread;
You seize the flower, the bloom is shed.

The best remedy for discontent
is to count our blessings.

It isn't our position but our disposition
that makes us happy.

By reading, I can exchange a dull hour
for a happy hour.

Employ life and you will enjoy life.

Wealth is not his that has it, but his that enjoys it.

I may be poor and have great riches.

Yes, it's pretty hard, the optimistic old woman admitted.
I have to get along with only two teeth—
one upper, one lower—but, thank goodness, they meet.

I do not feel any age yet.
There is no age to the spirit.

What sunshine is to flowers,
smiles are to humanity.

I want a soul so full of joy—
Life's withering storms cannot destroy.

So long as enthusiasm lasts,
so long is youth still with us.

It is good to let a little sunshine out
as well as in.

Growing old is no more
than a bad habit
which a busy person
has no time to form.

It takes both rain and sunshine
to make a rainbow.

The only way on earth to multiply happiness
is to divide it.

One of the best things a man can have up his sleeve
is a funny-bone.

People are lonely
because they build walls
instead of bridges.

The secret of being miserable
is to have the leisure to bother about
whether you are happy or not.

Just think how happy you'd be
if you lost everything you have right now—
and then got it back again.

When a man has a "pet peeve"
it's remarkable how often he pets it.

Things are pretty well evened up in this world.
Other people's troubles are not so bad as yours,
but their children are a lot worse.

Heaven is blessed with perfect rest,
but the blessing of earth is toil.

Better to light one candle
than to curse the darkness.

Humdrum is not where you live;
it's what you are.

If we learn how to give ourselves,
to forgive others, and to live with thanksgiving
we need not seek happiness—it will seek us.

A humorist is a man who feels bad
but feels good about it.

The load becomes light
which is cheerfully borne.

The days that make us happy make us wise.

Some men have their first dollar.
The man who is really rich
is one who still has his first friend.

He who has not forgiven an enemy has never yet tasted one of the most sublime enjoyments of life.

To speak kindly does not hurt the tongue.

Happiness is the only thing we can give
without having.

Happiness is not a station your arrive at,
but a manner of traveling.

All the flowers of all the tomorrows
are in the seeds of today.

If you don't get everything you want,
think of the things you don't get that you don't want.

Occupation is the necessary basis
of all enjoyment.

He enjoys much
who is thankful for little.

Happiness is not a reward—
it is a consequence.

He is happiest who finds his peace
in his home.

A smile is a curve
that can set a lot of things straight.

Few pleasures are more lasting
than reading a good book.

Sorrow, like rain, makes roses and mud.

Each new day is a chance
to start all over again.

The foolish man seeks
happiness in the distance;
the wise man grows it
under his feet.

I may be rich and have nothing.

Be cheerful, for of all the things you wear,
the look on your face is most important.

Happiness is in our own back yard.

Be the labor great or small—
Do it well or not at all.

We cannot have mountains
without valleys.

We can even smile through our tears if we try.

It isn't our position but our disposition
that makes us happy.

Happiness is a thing to be practiced
like a violin.

Laughter is the outward expression of joy.

I may be as happy in a cottage
as in a mansion.

peace

One who is afraid
of lying is usually
afraid of nothing else.

Worry never climbed a hill
Worry never paid a bill
Worry never dried a tear
Worry never calmed a fear
Worry never darned a heel
Worry never cooked a meal
Worry never led a horse to water
Worry never done a thing
you'd think it oughta.

The light that shows us our sin
is the light that heals us.

To be a seeker is soon to be a finder.

With God all things are possible.

If God be for me,
who can be against me?

The secret of contentment is know
how to enjoy what you have.

He that loves silver shall not be satisfied with silver;
nor he that loves abundance with increase.

All men desire peace;
few desire the things which make for peace.

Well-arranged time is the surest mark
of a well-arranged mind.

Few things are more bitter than to feel bitter.

There is no peace, says the Lord,
unto the wicked.

A clean conscience
is a soft pillow.

To carry care to bed is to sleep
with a pack on your back.

He that goes borrowing goes sorrowing.

Habit is man's best friend or his worst enemy.

Better is a handful with quietness, than both
the hands full with travail and vexation of spirit.

The fellow who worries about what
people think of him wouldn't worry so much
if he only knew how seldom they do.

Today, whatever may annoy
the word for me is *joy*, just simple joy.

In the keeping of God's commandments
there are great rewards,
and peace is only one of them.

Peace is not
the absence of conflict,
but the ability
to cope with it.

We cannot always control
what happens around us,
but we can control how we feel about it.

Don't hurry, don't worry,
Do your best, and leave the rest.

Life is like licking honey off a thorn.

In much of my talking, thinking is half-murdered.

Reality may be a rough road, but escape is a precipice.

The Bible is the book of all others to be read
at all ages and in all conditions of human life.

Pray for others.

You are none the holier
for being praised,
and none the worse
for being blamed.

Our restlessness is largely due to the fact
that we are as yet wanderers between two worlds.

He does not say,
"at the end of the way you find Me."
He says, "I AM the way:
I AM the road under your feet,
the road that begins just as low
as you happen to be."

He is only advancing in life whose heart is getting softer,
his blood warmer, his brain quicker,
and his spirit entering into living peace.

He who is taught to live upon little
owes more to his father's wisdom than he who has
a great deal left him does to his father's care.

It's right to be contented with what you have
but never with what you are.

Anger is a wind which blows
out the lamp of the mind.

Life is a voyage in which we choose
neither vessel nor weather, but much can
be done in the management of the sails
and the guidance of the helm.

To will what God wills brings peace.

Any housewife, no matter how large
her family, can always get some time
to be alone by doing the dishes.

Fear God and all other fears will disappear.

Pray or be a prey—
a prey to fears, to futilities, to ineffectiveness.

To be content with little is difficult,
to be content with much, impossible.

Be strong and of good courage;
be not afraid, neither be dismayed:
for the Lord your God is with you wherever you go.

Watching for riches consumes the flesh,
and the care thereof drives away sleep.

If I am at war
with myself,
I can bring little peace
to my fellow man.

If I trust in the Lord and do good,
I shall have a place to live and I shall be fed.

As long as man stands in his own way,
everything seems to be in his way.

The thing to put aside for one's old age
is all thought of retirement.

This is maturity:
To be able to stick with a job until it is finished;
to be able to bear an injustice without wanting to get even;
to be able to carry money without spending it;
and to do one's duty without being supervised.

Godliness with contentment is great gain.

The peace within becomes the harmony without.

I shall grow old, but never lose life's zest
Because the road's last turn will be the best.
Expect the best!

In solitude we are least alone.

How men treat us will make little difference when we know
we have God's approval.

Anger rests in the bosom of fools.

Every city or house divided against itself shall not stand.

As the heavens are higher than the earth,
so are God's ways higher than my ways and
God's thoughts are higher than my thoughts.

A minute of thought
is worth more than
an hour of talk.

gentleness

The merciful shall obtain mercy.

No man has it so good but that two or three words
can dishearten, and there is no calamity
but a few words can hearten.

Diplomacy is to do and say the nastiest thing
in the nicest way.

I have wept in the night
for the shortness of sight
That to somebody's need made me blind;
But I never have yet felt a twinge of regret
For being a little too kind.

The milk of human kindness
never curdles.

He who reforms himself
had done much
toward reforming others.

It is more blessed to give than to receive.

Today's profits are yesterday's goodwill ripened.

Punctuality is the politeness of kings
and the duty of gentle people everywhere.

A soft answer turns away wrath,
but grievous words stir up anger.

Be gentle to all people.

So many Gods, so many creeds.
So many paths that wind and wind;
When just the art of being kind
Is all the sad world needs.

Nothing is so strong
as gentleness,
nothing so gentle
as real strength.

An admission of error is a sign of strength
rather than a confession of weakness.

A merry heart does good like a medicine.

To every thing there is a season,
and a time to every purpose under the heaven.

Be to his virtues very kind.
Be to his faults a little blind.

Be kind, for everyone you meet
is fighting a hard battle.

We cannot always oblige,
but we can speak obligingly.

A small unkindness
is a great offense.

To listen well is as powerful a means
of influence as to talk well and is
as essential to all true conversation.

Man's inhumanity to man
makes countless thousands mourn.

Rejoice with them that do rejoice
and weep with them that weep.

Good manners are the small coin of virtue.

A noble heart, like the sun,
shows its greatest countenance in its lowest estate.

It is they who do their duties in everyday and
trivial matters who fulfill them on great occasions.

Culture is one thing and varnish another.

Let not the sun go down on your wrath.

To belittle is to be little.

What you dislike in another,
take care to correct in yourself.

A real friend is one who helps us to think
our noblest thoughts, put forth our best efforts,
and to be our best selves.

Withhold not good from them to whom it is due,
when it is in the power of your hand to do it.

If any man desires to be first,
the same shall be last of all, and servant of all.

A reproof means more to a wise man
than a hundred stripes to a fool.

He that hath mercy on the poor, happy is he.

When I think I stand, I should take heed lest I fall.

It were better for me that a millstone
were hanged about my neck, and that
I were drowned in the bottom of the sea,
than that I should offend a little one.

Add to your faith virtue; and to virtue
knowledge; and to knowledge temperance;
and to temperance patience; and to patience
godliness; and to godliness brotherly
kindness; and to brotherly kindness charity.

When you give your alms, do not sound
a trumpet before you, as the hypocrites do...
that they may have glory from men.

Let another man praise thee and not thine own mouth;
a stranger and not thine own lips.

When pride comes, then comes shame:
but with the lowly is wisdom.

The kindly word that falls today
may bear its fruit tomorrow.

Every noble life leaves the fibre of it interwoven
in the wool of the world.

True nobility comes of the gentle heart.

A gentleman is a gentle man.

The meek shall inherit
the earth; and shall
delight themselves in the
abundance of peace.

Be what you wish
others to become.

goodness

The highest reward for a man's toil
is not what he gets for it,
but rather what he becomes by it.

Praise not only pretends that we are better than we are;
it may help to make us better than we are.

We've got to build a better man
before we build a better society.

Silver and gold are not the only coin;
virtue also passes all over the world.

To every man there opens a high way and a low
and every man decides the way he shall go.

The smallest good deed is better
than the grandest good intention.

Character is a victory,
not a gift.

The hardest job that people have to do is to move religion from their throats to their muscles.

Though another may have more money, beauty, brains than you; yet when it comes to the rarer spiritual values such as charity, self-sacrifice, honor, nobility of heart, you have an equal chance with everyone to be the most beloved and honored of all people.

Children need models
before they need critics.

What you are in the sight of God,
that you truly are.

Be careful how you live; you may be the
only Bible some people will ever read.

Do right and
leave the results
with God.

I have resolved never to do anything
which I should be afraid to do
if it were the last hour of my life.

Give to him that asks you;
from him that would borrow of you
turn not away.

Can my creed be recognized in my deed?

Be what you say and say what you are.

Truth cannot be killed with the sword
nor abolished by law.

He that does good for good's sake
seeks neither praise nor reward,
but he is sure of both in the end.

Do good with what you have,
or it will do you no good.

Do unto others as though
you were the others.

If the cake is bad, what good is the frosting?

Legal immunity does not confer moral immunity.

Whosoever shall compel you to go a mile,
go with him two.

A good man leaves a good legacy
if he leaves his children educated.

I cannot serve two masters.

It shall be well with the righteous:
for they shall eat the fruit of their doing.

It shall be ill to the wicked:
for the reward of his hands shall be given to him.

To whom much is given, of him shall be much required.

No one has a right to do as he pleases,
except when he pleases to do right.

The eyes of the Lord are in every place
beholding the evil and the good.

If you want to put the world right,
start with yourself.

Life is not the wick
or the candle—
it is the burning.

If anyone speaks evil of you,
so live that none will believe it.

There is no right way to do the wrong thing.

The Devil has many tools,
but a lie is the handle that fits them all.

The earth is full of the goodness of the Lord.

We don't break God's laws—
we break ourselves on them.

Conscience is the still small voice
that makes you feel still smaller.

To him that knows to do good,
and does it not, to him it is a sin.

If the whole world followed you,
Followed to the letter,
Tell me—if it followed you,
Would the world be better?

A man is rich according to what he is,
not according to what he has.

Whatever I sow, that I shall reap.

You are not what
you think you are,
but you are
what you think.

You are not better for being praised
nor worse for being blamed.

Honest gain is the only permanent gain.

Pretty is as pretty does.

Oh, what a tangled web we weave,
when first we practice to deceive.

The rung of a ladder was never meant to rest upon,
but only to hold a man's foot long enough
to enable him to put the other one higher.

Whosoever shall smite you on your right cheek,
turn to him the other also.

He who walks with wise men shall be wise:
but a companion of fools shall be destroyed.

Honesty is always the best policy.

It is better to suffer for speaking the truth
than that the truth should suffer
for want of speaking it.

The only way to settle
a disagreement is on the
basis of what's right—
not who's right.

The measure of a man's real character
is what he would do if he knew
he would never be found out.

Whatever is worth doing at all,
is worth doing well.

Better is a little with righteousness
than great revenues without right.

There may be times
when you cannot find help,
but there is not time
when you cannot give help.

We have committed the Golden Rule to memory;
let us now commit it to life.

There is so much good in the worst of us,
and so much bad in the best of us,
that it behooves all of us
not to talk about the rest of us.

Truth is the foundation of all knowledge
and the cement of all societies.

He who is not liberal
with what he has
deceives himself
when he thinks
he would be liberal
if he had more.

The world is slowly learning that because two
men think different neither need be wicked.

Nothing which is morally wrong
can ever be politically right.

It is often surprising to find what heights may
be attained merely by remaining on the level.

The Devil has many tools,
but a lie is the handle that fits them all.

The wicked borrows, and pays not again:
but the righteous shows mercy and gives.

One sinner destroys much good.

He who covers his sins shall not prosper: but whoso confesses and forsakes them shall have mercy.

Truth cannot be killed with the sword or gun nor abolished by law.

There is no better exercise
for strengthening the heart
that reaching down
and lifting people up.

The hand that's dirty
with honest labor
is fit to shake
with any neighbor.

Jo Petty was the well known author
of many inspirational books
including APPLES OF GOLD and
WINGS OF SILVER. Her classic books
of inspiration have been sought by
millions of enthusiastic readers. She died
in 2007 at nearly 100 years of age.